My Love, My Seasons

My Love, My Seasons

Tapan Pattanaik

Translated from the Odia by
Dr. Namita Laxmi Jagaddeb

BLACK EAGLE BOOKS
2019

 BLACK EAGLE BOOKS

7464 Wisdom Lane
Dublin, OH 43016
E-mail: info@blackeaglebooks.org
Website: www.blackeaglebooks.org

First US edition published by
BLACK EAGLE BOOKS, 2019

My Love, My Seasons by Tapan Pattanaik

Translation by **Dr. Namita Laxmi Jagaddeb**

Copyright of original © **Tapan Pattanaik**
Copyright translation © **Dr. Namita Laxmi Jagaddeb**

All rights reserved. No part of this publication may be reproduced, stored in a retrieval system, or transmitted, in any form or by any means, electronic, mechanical, photocopying, recording or otherwise without the prior permission of the publisher.

Cover and Interior Design: Ezy's Publication

DTP: Khusi Graphics, Bapuji Nagar, Bhubaneswar

Library of Congress Control Number: 2019939703
ISBN- 978-1-64560-009-1 (Paperback)

Printed in United States of America

Dedicated
To
Lord Jagannath,
The Almighty

Acknowledgement

I owe my deep debt of gratitude to Shri Jayanta Mahapatra, the great poet and translator of Odisha (India), his "ancient love of a hundred names", who, inspite of his indisposition read my translation work with "a great deal of pleasure" and conveyed his impression in such intimate terms as has stirred me profoundly. A recipient of Central Sahitya Academi award, along with many prestigious international honours, Shri Mahapatra is considered to be one of the best and most prolific Indian English poets of the post-independence era. The humble, nonagenarian poet appears unstoppable in his poetic odyssey.

I am deeply grateful to Shri Haraprasad Das, the illustrious poet, critic, columnist of Odisha (India), who, apart from giving me valuable advice on literary matter, has been kind enough to convey his highly significant observation on my work that has validated my endeavour. Shri Das, a Central Sahitya Sahitya Academi awardee, is well known for his insightful views on life, literature and culture. A great myth-maker and thinker of our times. His guidance which I very often seek, has always been enlightening to me.

I am extremely thankful to Muhammad Shanazar(Meph.),

one of the most sought-after poets of the world today, for having read my work and recorded his kind observation, terming it a "superb gift". Md. Shanazar is adorned with more than 50 prestigious international awards and honours as a poet, translator and ambassador for peace by reputed organizations across the globe. His creative passion for love, peace and fellowship through literature has always inspired me.

I sincerely acknowledge my indebtedness to my teacher and a notable English poet, Prof. (Dr) Ram Narayan Panda, PG Deptt. of English, Berhampur University (Odisha), who, in addition to providing very useful suggestions, has taken much pains to write a perceptive foreword in appreciation of this work.

My special gratitude is due to my "Gurudev" Prof. Abhinna Chandra Sahu, the renowned Odia poet, critic and educationist, who has been an everlasting source of inspiration to me, in my literary mission in general and this work in particular.

I am sincerely thankful to Shri Satya Pattanaik, the US based poet of reputation and publisher of Black Eagle, who readily agreed to publish this work of mine with a whole-heartedness that surprised me.

Finally, Shri Tapan Pattanaik, the poet; the originator of my work, deserves my deep gratitude. The poet, despite his prolonged illness never fails to cheer me. Shri Pattanaik has been writing non-stop for over the last five decades. A wonderful poetic personae; for him poetry is life, life poetry.

Dr. Namita Laxmi Jagaddeb

Foreword

My Love, My Seasons is the translated version of Rutura Basnare, a lovely anthology of Odia poems by Tapan Pattanaik, one of the distinguished Odia poets of the contemporary period. This volume is predominantly a collection of poems, mostly lyrics, dwelling on the themes of love and longing intertwined with a myriad of issues of timeless significance such as loneliness, Nature, and renunciation.

Even in the translated version, the original author's creativity registers its authenticity in terms of both form and substance. Interestingly, the mimetic dimension, involving description of Nature, Chilika for instance, is never divested of an emotional, and even at times, a philosophical component. In other words, mimeticism is more often than not used as a means to an end, that is, achieving strong emotional and/or philosophical statements, in spite of the fact that the use of varied imagery helps construct an armature of sensuousness. This is significantly true of Keats' description of the season in the iconic poem "To Autumn."

The first poem titled "Chilika in Season's Mirror" is the most representative poem of this volume employing in a Keatsian as well as Yeatsian fashion, dualities of different kinds: Transience/Permanence, Beauty/Truth, Terrestrial/Eternal, Phenomenal/ Noumenal, to name a few.

In addition to that, there is a distinct humanization of Nature, almost the way that Thomas Hardy does by way of using Nature as mirroring the poet's consciousness. A supreme example of this metaphoricity of Nature is noticed in the following lines:

> Chilika is solitary, utterly alone,
> tears well up in her eyes,
> as if someone whispers to her:
> "You are fated to walk
> the life by yourself
> singing along a sad song
> all the way."(p.2)

Even though the poet invests Chilika with his own loneliness, he is aware of the fact that, unlike himself, the lake stands out as a symbol of eternity, re-enacting the age-old tension between "timeless" and "temporal":

> Myriad dawns and dusks
> are dead through a million births;
> she has kept scores of sagas
> of bygone eras close to her heart
> as cherished treasure. (p.2)

Even the poet makes no secret of his dismay at the subjugation of the lake to the present-day commercial opportunism. Hence, there is an unmistakable echo of the Yeatsian lamentation "That is no country for old men" ("Sailing to Byzantium," line 1) in the following lines:

> Here in this world
> life is an item for trade;

it has no rhyme no rhythm,
a clay toy only,
in the hands of man. (p.2)

The poems dramatize a paradox involving co-existence of longing for eternity and preoccupation with the world of the senses, or beauty. But, this paradox is subsequently resolved as the translator rightly notes: "At times, the poet yearns to live beyond the cycle of seasons, but, nevertheless, he favours a life lost in seasons." Needless to mention, for the poet, "ä thing of beauty is a joy forever" (Keats, Endymion)

On the whole, this is a volume of poems, translated fairly well, capturing man's obvious infatuation for the beauty of Nature, eternal yearning for love, combined with natural abhorrence to loneliness, and a desire for select companionship. Hence, basically dejected owing to "bewildered love" (p.9), the poet automatically finds life "ä carnival of nothingness" (p.9) on the one hand. On the other, the poet perforce defines renunciation only in terms of the many shades of life:

. . . Renunciation is a memoir
on numerous attainments. (p.9)

This is more or less in line with Keats' description of "Melancholy": "She dwells with Beauty; Beauty that must die" (Keats, "Ön Melancholy" L. 21). Thus, the poet's disenchantment with the world of senses is predominantly felt throughout the poems. But, it is coupled with a strong assertion of an unmitigated zest for life, warts and all.

Prof. (Dr) Ram Narayan Panda
PG Deptt. of English
Berhampur University (Odisha)

Dr. Namita Laxmi Jagaddeb As Translator

Luckily I had an opportunity to see the English translation of Shri Tapan Pattanaik's Poems of Rutura Basnare. The poems have been accomplished by Dr. Namita Laxmi Jagaddeb; she translated from Odia into English. Though I confess I have little knowledge of Odia, yet beauty and flow in translation stunned me and I could help commenting on the translation work of Dr. Namita Laxmi Jagaddeb. I too translated several poets and writers and have gone through multifarious issues, the foremost feeling that I have experienced, is that creative work is easier than its translation for the reason that a poet or a writer enjoys himself a creative freedom or independence for expression of thoughts and feelings but the translator is restricted, he or she has least independence for the translator has to stick very close to which has been written in original langue. Besides; the quality of negative capability is indispensable for the translator, he or she has to adapt himself to the state of mind in which the genuine works have been written, else the translator can't interpret sentiments of the writer being translated; therefore, the translator has to observe at the same time all intricacies and delicacies which bring the translation to original work. Joseph Brodsky says, "Translation is not original creation - that is what one must remember. In translation, some loss is inevitable." Another writer Kate Grenville comments on translation, "Each language has its own take on the world. That's why a translation can never be absolutely exact, and therefore, when you enter another language and speak with its speakers, you become a slightly different person; you learn a different sort of world."

I have gone through several poems translated by Dr. Namita Laxmi Jagaddeb and found spirit of the work quite intact and striking. The very first poem "Chilika In Seasons" made me feel as if it was created originally in English, because the translator did not stifle live images of the poem. She transmitted its imagery with all its shades and colours with the same features. The whole poem has been translated with superb lucidity:

Here in this world/Life is an item of trade/It has no rhyme no rhythm/A clay toy only,

In the hands of man/Life is frozen in a frame of glass...

Dr. Namita Laxmi Jagaddeb, being a translator, time and again, dissolves her identity which is distinctively a female and reassembles herself into the entity of the poet being translated who by gender s a male and grasps his sentiments and feelings to put on them a new costume and it is a quite challenging job. She splendidly transmuted the beautiful feelings expressed in 'Lamp of Love' which evidenced that the translator did neither scratch nor bumped the delicate eggs of thoughts while changing their cases, she handled them with utmost care:

Everything will go as usual/Cycle of season/Renewal dreams/Rivers menstruating/Sea holding anniversaries/ Butterflies chairing/The assembles of flowers/On the river isles/Yet I must wait/Where I am, to keep on burning/ The lamp of love/Till you come back to me/For I will plant the sweet bloom/On your coiffured crown.

Most of all the translator used with utmost precision grammatical correct language which enhances worth of the translated work, besides, common poetic diction has been used, grandiloquence has been avoided, impacts of the work have been kept alive and healthy, the translator did not let blur genuine grace and shine of the original work. Just see how poetic diction has been picked in the poem 'Life':

The pallid twilight/Slowly washes colours/Off the weary earth/By sprinkling dust/Celestial canvass mellows./Someone gets down/With brush and colours/ To paint the memoir of night/But, alas! The wintry night of pausha/Is, only, vacant and dull.

The translator kept intact visual and pictorial imagery with a great caution and it is an evidence of her astuteness in the field of translation:

Life keeps floating here and there/Like a banyan leaf till it rots/And sticks somewhere.

Life saunters on/As if an innocent lamb toddling/ Holding the hand of Time.

Dr. Namita Laxmi Jagaddeb, after translating the work of Shiri Tapan Pattanaik, gave it a new costume, broader and wider scope, she smashed the regional boundaries of its confinement and brought it into global arena, her efforts made these magnificent pieces a part of living literature, it is a superb gift for the fans and critics of poetry, she has made it easy for those who want to delve into the heart and mind of Shri Tapan Pattanaik. My utmost regards, respect and love for Dr. Namita Laxmi Jagaddeb.

Muhammad Shanazar (Meph.)
Internationally recognised English Poet and Translator of Pakistan

Jayanta Mahapatra

On "My Love, My Seasons" by Tapan Patnaik
Translated from the Odia by Namita Laxmi Jagaddeb

TIME is the mover behind Tapan Patnaik's story. It is a story of what time does to us as it keeps "hurtling ahead / from one station to the other / passengers getting in and out / as if a house on fire." Tapan Patnaik's acute perception of time continues throughout almost all the poems in this collection of poetry. Pitifully aware that "Amazing is the tide of time / its origin known to none," ("Moment by Moment"), he observes the contentment of "the weaving bird / the nest tossing in the wind" while "life is squeezed into infinity / like ink sink (ing) through blotting paper" ("Moment by Moment").

Beautiful imagery!
But it is not only about life and its vicissitudes that come through the poems. The fascination with the notion that our existence itself cannot leave us ever alone, opens up questions for him. This is from his poem "Experience":

> "All of them,
> Life, Soul, ... when merge,
> Into worn-out pages of heart's manuscript,
> Tells the story of bewildered love
> that produces a broken world..."

The poet, whose life with its broken and unbroken days, is spent on the shores of the scenic, undefiled lake Chilika, tears through his own lonely existence with lines such as:

> "Chilika is solitary, utterly alone,
> Tears well up in her eyes,
> as if someone whispers to her:
> You are fated to walk
> the life by yourself
> Singing along a sad song
> all the way."

"Chilika in Seasons' Mirror"

Jayanta Mahapatra

Page 2, continued

I read with a great deal of pleasure these thoughtful and lyrically made poems in Namita Laxmi's manuscript. Namita has a restraint and a care for craftsmanship which renders the Odia poems of Tapan Patnaik welcome and accessible. I'm sure these translations will be of much interest for non-Odia readers of this sensitive Odia poet.

Finally, I'd like to say that "My Love, My Seasons" is quite effective in drawing strong pictures of the human condition.

April 7, 2019   Jayanta Mahapatra

Translator's Note

The poet Tapan Pattanaik needs no introduction, he being one of the most prolific and popular writers of contemporary Odia literature. His ceaseless literary pursuit for over five decades has made him a role model for many a blooming talent of the younger generations.

The fifty poems which I have translated are taken from his Odia anthology of poems entitled 'Rutura Basnare' published in 2003. To my mind, the poet here is at his creative best and most akin to his soul. A virtual masterpiece, wherein the poet celebrates life in Nature at the backdrop of a fugitive Time. With seasons appear, disappear and reappear, poet's cup of life gets filled to the brim with sweetness and light. Yet, he feels like losing out to Time, the inevitable and the relentless. This perhaps accounts for a deep sense of pathos and nostalgia underlying most of his poems. At times, the poet yearns to live beyond the cycle of seasons, but, nevertheless, he favours a life lost in seasons.

The poems are hallmarked with densely textured metaphors and brilliant images handpicked by the poet from the countryside which he loves most. The lyrical intensity is invariably animated by a free flowing rhythm coupled with a supple diction used by the rural folk.

I am fortunate that the poet chose me to render 'Rutura Basnare' into English which I humbly accepted knowing fully well that translating Tapan Pattanaik is by no means an easy task. But, to my surprise, as I sat to go ahead, I felt exalted and went on working on poem after poem with a wonderful speed, ease and resilience I never expected. The entire exercise is a sincere endeavour undertaken in honour of the celebrated author. In my venture to recapture the lyrical utterance of the poet, I have taken utmost care to retain the beauty and flavour of the original.

I fervently hope, the readers will find my work enjoyable and engaging, too.

Dr. Namita Laxmi Jagaddeb

CONTENTS

Chilika, the Seasons' Mirror	25
Lamp of Love	29
A Tearful Song	31
River	32
Experience	33
A strange Psyche	35
Life	36
The Silent Flow of Life	38
In Service of Life	40
Portrait of a Monsoon Girl in the Palace of Khalikote	42
Your Village in a Moonlit Night	44
The Last Evening of Pausha	46
Astamee Chanda	48
Zone to Zone	50
Identity	52
The Spoilt Dream	54
The Poet	56
From Sunshine to Star	57
The Blank Page	59
The Perimeter	60
Pervasiveness	62
The Winter Night	65

The Tenure of Time	67
The Imagery	69
Krushna Chandra Tripathy	71
A Lonely Story	73
A Song for Season	75
Surrender	76
Life Petering out	78
The Waning Hour	79
The Role	80
The Solace	82
Indifference	83
The River of Wishes	84
History	86
The Omniscient	88
Life at the Tail End	89
No Answer	90
The Caution	91
The Hug	92
The Notice	94
The Poetic Person	95
The House of Illusion	96
Role Play	98
The Touch	100
Moment to Moment	101
Pyramid	103
Saluting the Century	105
The Self	107
Amid the Scented Seasons	109

*CHILIKA IN SEASONS' MIRROR

What a wide azure elegant sky,
caught lovely in a painting
on the bosom of Chilika lake!
A virtual landscape on water playing
hide and seek with sun and shade,
moon and stars,
a carnival of colours, as it were.

How thrilling!
Chilika is quick in switching hues
in turns between blue and grey,
murky and gold
as tides surge and plunge
in rotations.
Sometimes, she goes wild and
then falls quiet and serene.

The visiting birds,
her countless sweethearts
keep on ringing melancholy notes;
mountains, too, look on with moist eyes
as thick winter moves slowly
kissing and caressing her.
Chilika is solitary, utterly alone,
Tears well up in her eyes,
as if someone whispers to her:
you are fated to walk
the life by yourself
singing along a sad song
all the way.

Myriad dawns and dusks
are dead through a million births;
she has kept a scores of sagas
of bygone eras close to her heart
as cherished treasure.
Time and again, she has tested life
for pearls of love, but failed
and cried like a beggar maid.

Here in this world
life is an item for trade;
it has no rhyme no rhythm,
a clay toy only,
in the hands of man,
life is frozen in a frame of glass.
Is it shivering chill,
or someone smears dew drops

on her body with cool thrill
of sandal wood paste!
Chilika grooms herself as a bride,
her coiffured crown,
smells **Kia Ketaki;
but, she shudders at the sight
of moon alone in sky
fearing the moon would come down
skip and leap on her soft bosom
and ask for varied things.

She sobs quietly by the waves,
fancies the idea of gifting a boat
which would emanate
a wistful gazal:
The world is elusive,
belongs to none.
Someone would be on fire on the pyre
on the shore
by the tumbling grave.

Change of season
changes the panorama,
patterns of colour of
charming Chilika;
yet, leaves behind traces of life
hard to follow.
Now is time, Hansarali birds
fly back singing to ***Mana Sarobara
past the high peaks
of ****Mamu Bhanaja.

Chilika lies in wait
for rotation of season
and her metamorphosis
into an angelic beauty.

A large brackish water lagoon along the sea coast of Odisha; a favourite destination of migratory birds and tourists.
**Screw pine plants, thorny long leafed shrubs bearing strong scented flowers.*
***Mana Sarobara - A Himalayan lake having mythical significance.*
****Mamu Bhanaja - Legendary twin hills on the bank of Chilika lake.*

LAMP OF LOVE

You wished to lit up a lamp for you
but did not tell me,
how long, for how many lives
I would keept it burning.
Words will metmorphose
into mountations of which
tearful rivers will flow down
and carry the paper boats
made by you
narrating our tales
far and wide.

Everything will go on as usual ;
cycle of seasons,
renewal dreams,
rivers menstruating,

sea holding anniversaries,
butterflies chairing
the assemblies of flowers
on the river isles;
yet, I must wait
where I am, to keep on burning
the lamp of love
till you come back to me
for I will plant the sweet blooms
on your coiffured crown.

A TEARFUL SONG

How can I compose a tearful song
at this shady, enchanting hour,
when soul's estate is tangled
in nets of thousand sorrows?

The beggar man's life sinks
beneath his doleful fiddle,
but swells the river of melancholy
whose song rocks my boat violently.
Yet, I have to navigate the life
amid unending anguish.

Oh, God !
I was utterly unaware ;
or else,
I would have prayed earnestly
not to create me
a soft tearful song.

RIVER

A full moon in the dark of night
a fistful gloom in the moon-lit glow

River begs for stars,
fair as ridge gourd blooms;
begs for golden beams
in the glistening morn.

River begs from earth,
begs for life,
begs from humans,
this thing, that thing
as is her wont.

River keeps on gliding
hugging a bunch of gulmohars,
her lips trembling by the slanted sun,
heart reaching out to a nameless bird
singing passionately a meloncholy tune
at the foot of a tree on the shore.

EXPERIENCE

Life is a carnival of nothingness,
but, soul, a sweet symphony
of myriad consciousness.
Detachment is the final yield
of a lot of love making;
while Renunciation is a memoir
on numerous attainments;
Sacrifice of copious dreams
begets Burning.

All of them,
the Life, the Soul, Detachment,

Renunciation, Burning when merge into
worn out pages of heart's manuscripts,
tells the story of bewildered love
that produces a broken world
with a shattered sky,
a handful of stars,
a glow of laughter,
an erratic gale.

The womb of night is now filled with
pearls of dew,
let's come together
with moist lips
and sing a wistful gazal.

A STRANGE PSYCHE

A lyric of swelling grief
penned in tears of cloud
animates rain, summer
spring and winter.

Summer burns, rains soak;
memories appear and disappear quietly.
Sun's rising, moon's sinking,
like someone losing, looking around
and erecting a flight of stairs
from earth to heaven.

The far-off song of a way farerer
like a night bird stays awake.
In a moment, a storm
plagues the sky;
while someone keeps on singing
the song of life
from night to morn
in a strange manner.

No one knows who is
burning within.

LIFE

The pallid twilight
slowly washes colours
off the weary earth
by sprinkling dust,
celestial canvass mellows.
Someone gets down
with brush and colour
to paint the memoir of night,
but, alas! the wintry night of *pausha
is, only, vacant and dull.

When moon bends over the hill
and hill on the bosom of the river,
sweet memories of our lovely night
enchant me, my whole being;
I forget every other thing.

The scented **ketaki
kisses me softly,
as night shifts colour
on the lonely bed of sand,
on the wings of fatigued birds.
I will arise and go now,

to meet my sweet heart
hopping over numerous turns and lanes far away
where she waits my arrival
for years on end.

Life, for her, is suffering,
only suffering.

*Month of Winter
**Screw pine plants, thorny long leafed shrubs
bearing strong scented flowers.

THE SILENT FLOW OF LIFE

While telling the story
the book is half done
as soul's dialogues
not easy to capture.

Quiet flows the life;
its beginning and end
known to none.
None knows
how far it flows, where.
It moves on and on, far off
from one end to other of the world.

Life keeps on floating here and there
like a banyan leaf till it rots
and sticks somewhere.
Life saunters on
as if an innocent lamb toddling,
holding hand of Time.

Silent current runs ahead
sweeping all in its sway;
sun and shadows and paddies;

clouds' hide and seek in spring;
the hour of profound sorrow;
dark night of Pausha, lonesome wind
and the idle songs of sensitive dews.

Someone is busy building castle
on his own grave
knowing not what may happen to him
the next moment.

While writing this epilogue on life,
the book is half done.
None has ever uttered the last word
till date.

The flow of life moves on silently.
Only a baffling song
is heard from some vacant zone.

IN SERVICE OF LIFE

Passions flee breaking
the barricades of time;
whirlwind sweeps
tender leaves of life.

Pause and observe
the ascent and descent
of sun and moon who reveal
the strange ways of time,
marvels of life and death.

Someone has departed
lighting a lamp of love
for a powerful poem to spring
in the life to come.

The aura of salvation elongates
from earth to heaven.
Poet is unerring;
sin or curse not his due.
He is a great achiever,
admits no full stop
in serving the life.

Look!
His dwelling is the vacant sky,
there he keeps on glowing the lamp
of love and steadfastness.

PORTRAIT OF A MONSOON GIRL IN THE PALACE OF *KHALIKOTE

Countless lyrics came crowding me
as I gazed at the royal palace of Khilikote,
in a state of repose amid mountains
laden with stacks of cloud,
heaps of matted bush.
While rains roaring
like a fierce python;
silent was the rock
grave and solid
like a dark night.

Time rotates the cycle of seasons;
Rains come each year,
but rains not only rain,
at times, it turns
rain of tears.

The aged woman in the palace
reminded me her life,
a youth sacrificed,
a living Konark, a dumb witness
to devotion steeped in sorrow.

The poet's daughter
in the gallery of art
beckoned me.
As I drew near,
she stepped out briskly
and began reciting
poems lit up by Time,
and instantly, I shot back
to hundred years only to sense:
Renewal of Being, the essence of Life,
Time shuttling, a mediator only.

The image then began to ooze colour
like pearls of tear.
The art was old, not dead.

*The royal headquarters of an ex-princely state of Odisha.

YOUR VILLAGE
IN A MOONLIT NIGHT

In the moonlit night
the train is zooming;
rivers, bridges, canals, paddies
leaving behind,
the train is racing.

Now, your lovely face flashed
in the vacant sky and lingered;
you tiptoed through the window,
sat, by my side and sang
in a thrilling voice
the song you used to sing,
and then fled without a word into moonlit air.
The train is still whistling ahead.

In a moment, your little cottage appeared
at the end of the hamlet
amid Sal forest;
Bagul trees lining up
the green hill;
your sweet home pecked
in moon light and vanished;

oh, my golden girl,
I am pining for you.

As I am racing past your hamlet
I hear you beckon me
from the hills, from the river,
from far and near.
My soul is stirred.

I truly believe, you are with me;
you, the girl lost in yourself,
keeps on calling me
and calling me.

THE LAST EVENING OF *PAUSHA

Up, above a cloudless sky,
below, down a mat of grass;
songs of reapers
resound the fields,
vibrate the air.

Gathering chill shivers the body
but daren't shake the life of grace,
of action and thought.

Dusk alights gently
on mustard fields
kissing tiny flowers,
caressing golden dust of village lane
and rippling water of the pond.

The evening ritual begins
with jingling of anklets
of the little feet,
loud chanting of hymns
and deafening gong
in the sanctum sanctorum.

Community halls are no more
the pride of villages,
cacophonous bizarre songs
now rule the roost.
As evening mellows,
the virgin moon floats up
clearing mirror of the village
with fresh dews.
None knows who longs for whom,
whose look is revealed in whose eyes,
only moon is the witness.
Someone's laugh radiates
with the glean of coconut trees,
while another's tears
plunge the house next door.

For someone,
the last evening of Pausha
glows like a lamp of bliss;
for the other,
life ceases in the lump of
collyrium tear,
pining, trying, testing
all the way.

---

* *A month of winter; the lunar month corresponding to the period between middle of December to middle of January.*

*ASHTAMEE CHANDA

Night mellows,
the wind loiters naked here and there ;
Ashtamee Chanda
begins spraying pink;
the ghost of my past weakens me
and I see you appear
furtively and slowly
while poetic lines lie scattered
in casuarina gleam.

We did not ask anything each other.
Night birds twittered something,
broke the hushed silence,
nothing was revealed
of the heart of the matter.
Thus, some ventured
to think of writing theses,
but all of the maladies not amenable
to ayurveda or allopathy.

In the days, gone by,
we used to sit side by side
cajoling, laughing, sharing

the intimate story and dialogues
of our life.
The same story, we too read
on the portals of temples;
the saga of man's rise and fall,
deduction and division
of the same arithmetic.
The sun and moon
hide out each other, yet linger on.
Who can prolong
the assigned hour to play out the role,
to sing so long?

After many a century
I am born again.
I see the same moon, the same stars,
the same blossoming Kashatandi,
the same whispering voices
beneath the casuarinas.
Age has not withered,
nothing has changed
barring some flesh, bone, blood and fat.
Soul lies intact; the boat of life
moves ahead slowly yet steadily.

You reappeared the same way
furtively, unhurriedly
to the rhythm of poetic lines,
glittering under the canopy
of tamarisk trees.

Moon of the eighth day of a lunar fortnight.

ZONE TO ZONE

Multihued impassive birds
line up the sky,
break the silence
tweeting some magical notes.
Blue tides surge
with strange, inspiring music;
all anguish melt;
dismissing the sorrows and sufferings,
man walks on.

Absurd is man;
he laughs and weeps, in turns
all the while, yet keeps on moving.

Salute to Time, the ever present,
rest is ephemeral.
Light and darkness
whisper each other,
for life is the symphony of love
the living bond between them.
A fatigued traveller
along the long meandering path
dreams that sweetens the mind

and moves on.
That flow sing all the time
while sailing the boats
of many a soul
to some far-off zone.

IDENTITY

Time has told
many a stunning story
of centuries vanishing,
empires falling
and stored with care
layers of myriad dreams, souvenirs
and traces of footprints
in the clutch bag.
Ocean is asleep quietly
amid shells and oysters

Time lives on phenomena,
yet, tucked away casually
many of them into dark corners:
brahmins, scholars, scriptures,
diamonds, pearls, Queens' ivory beds
to Kings' hunting escapades.

Exit or entry
is irrelevant to Time.
Not a single trace
lingers long on its ruthless body.
shattering all illusion

erasing all identities
the ruthless time
renews and reveals the true self.

THE SPOILT DREAM

So many nights I passed
in vague thoughtfulness,
so many days in intimate companionship,
so many dreams lay waste
on this doleful sky,
lots of tales and fables,
ended in memories, frail and faded.

Even the night sky wept
shedding tears of dew,
star lamps flickered,
temple dancers got tired comforting her.
Plenty of words and dialogues
passed in between; went unheard
in the witching hour of night.

None could sense
the world was profound;
some crowed about their feats
and deeds; words multiplied
like jingle of anklets,
sweet music of the flow of time
stunned humanity.

This is the journey of life,
starts here only but finished already.
No one cares;
man is a straw in the wind
left with little learning
always at the beck and call of Time;
an obedient pupil, as it were.

The quiet Time is the final arbiter ;
life's voyage by the courtesy of Time.

THE POET

Oh, the lingering damsel,
in a painted posture,
bashful eyes, plaited palms,
lost in thoughts for aeons on end;
yet, numerous slaps of waves
thrill your body.

Wind and casuarinas chitchat
in a hissing voice,
in a language of their own.
All talks tend to be queer;
carry the image of life in dream.
What form when overwhelm
the time, person and place!
Nothing is known to him.
He is a poet.

While groping for life within you,
the poet gets buried unaware,
beneath nameless heaps of Time.

FROM SUNSHINE TO STAR

The sun, after a long day's journey
has sunk beyond the hills;
margin of the sky
is painted orange red;
rhapsodic moon
has begun playing with
ancient melody
on the glaze of sea water.
Perched on
glistening casurinas,
night birds gaze on
with beautiful ethereal eyes,
as zig zag dooms of sand
kiss the lips of ocean.

Below the bubbling foam
beauty of shells and oysters;
a lot of toing and froing,
nothing but trade,
only bargaining
a price for life.

Lamp of life flickers,
joys and sorrows,
smiles and tears
drop like pearls.
The fleeting life appears
and flees quickly.

THE BLANK PAGE

Beneath the bright sky,
earth is matted green,
river layered blue;
time racing non-stop
piercing human passion
to the core.

May be in a while
I would be no more
for this lovely sight ;
desires would have gone
the way of all flesh,
none would be here
to see the light of the morn
for which a war of words
is raised today.

This moon, these stars
offer deadly desires to live,
but life is a blank page.
What is amusing is
only flux and fiction.

THE PERIMETER

Mark the waning moon, wilting bodies
and dews dripping ;
all are ruthless traces
of a tyrant Time.

River flows through hamlets and woods
not knowing their names;
birds sing not knowing
the melody, rhyme or rhythm.
They don't care to know
which century when declined,
fell or doomed.

Moonlit nights, pearls of dew
have composed so many gazals
on unknown tears;
life's blues wing their way
to remote stars;
flowers smell sweet,
sun shines and sets,
night sits pretty,
opening out fairy tales
from grandama's pack.

A young body is afire
on live pyre;
subtle yearnings
stay behind.
The dying moon weeps
over the blurred horizon,
when a ruddy goose proclaims:
Life is arid, yet, amazing.

For whom all the fun, all the role plays!
Whatever vainly he carries
in the camel belley
will one day kick out
of his tiny mindset.

PERVASIVENESS

Like alphabets blur into darkness,
someone enters and exits anonymous
without uttering a single word
and turned into a stream of dew.

Flow of Time is like
a naughty boy's wilful ways,
never listens to appeal for halt,
a windstorm, as it were.

No one knows,
the whirlwind of Time
will shut down the shops without warning
and shatter lives driving all
into false love and charm
and write stories on many a life,
walking along the beach of the world.
No one knows the way in
and the way out;
where to sit, how long
to count the waves.

To lodge in the world is
to hit and run,
to run and play,
to seize things, buy and sell;
The sea will, one day, surge in billows,
breaching the sand bar;
nothing but the empty tunes
of shehnai will be heard.

Once the show is over
Time will not keep count of
who enters, who retires.

Spring and flowers are ablaze;
moon and stars have composed
many a lyric for the river ;
winter mist too sang
so many wilted songs.
Numerous tales written on foiled love
triggers the charmed dialogues of youth.

Strayed birds twitter
in buoyant twilight,
drops of hot tear trickle down
now and then.

the book lies unfinished,
while ruminating thus
the diverse ways of life
ever stretching;
for which moon, the night is too long
for which sun, the day is so pervasive,

so prolonged
the silent Time fails to contain.

Flowers bloom in the garden of life
in multiple hues
only to wither quietly.
One may see or shut off eyes
to this truth of life;
Time keeps on saying
the same thing
over and again.

THE WINTER NIGHT

Winter has arrived,
penning unending lyrics
on the song book of heart,
drawing a picture perfect
with tearful ink.
It's no dream, but a live icon
utmost sacred.

Body is brimmed with warm feelings,
heart with grief inconsolable,
her haunting memories
ringing all around
for the love is not earthly
nor fated to die.

Butterflies of varied colours
born of imagination
throng the garden of heart;
cool evening rolls out
moon's flowery beams
nestling us in a warm hug;
an unbreakable bond as it were,
between flower and butterfly.

THE TENURE OF TIME

All my queries fell flat,
for the boy is naughty;
its name is Time,
fond of sitting alone
below the water way
at the end of the village;
gleefully watches the blue sky
and brown earth ;
the ascent and descent
of sun and moon
life after life.

Life is fascinating
for its rarity and varieties;
its sweetness and beauty that bind all
with a powerful cord of love.

The current of Time has long life
It neither flees you
nor dwells with you.
Like a willful boy
it plays with the song of wind
amid green moss gathering

under bathing steps;
at times, grows furious,
and flies instantly with wings spread out
shooting into remote horizon
far beyond the sea.

The quiet flow of Time
sporting a lot of soft grey images
on its feathers, keeps on chanting hymns
of some pitiable souls.
Beneath the feeble light
the fatigued body fades,
Time forgets all faces
all persons, near and dear ones.

THE IMAGERY

Here was a stream,
used to listen to songs
of moon and stars,
while the scented earth
luring the sky ;
wind, too, murmured
a solitary tune.
Now, nothing is seen;
only a handful of ashes
and awful silence.

Someone buries the treasures of the day
with a scattering of flowers,
but goes on strewing
the memories of bygone eras.
Man is apt to forget the present,
like the desire for body
one loves and neglects.

In a game of waiting,
followed by apathy
auspicious hour never shows up;
memories grow hazier

beneath an anemic moon;
even in your absence
you get to me;
I, too, join with you quietly.

In the moment of reunion
we never recall
how one day
while sizzling in agonizing pain
we lost each other.

For days, months, years on end,
a soul pining for
the spring and the rains
will rise again
after several births
to be one with the other.

*KRUSHNA CHANDRA TRIPATHY

Oh, the unique soul,
a rare happening on earth;
your heart's portal,
serene and pure
never opened up
for tricks and deceits.

Even today,
gale brews over Chilika,
gathering darkness;
packs of Era and Gendalia
huddle together
on the hill top of Jatia.

Even today, the beggar boy
treads his way to a far-off town;
bamboo groves of Solari
quiver at the wet footfalls
of a widow.
But, the poet is silent;
the memorial emanates
his moving lyrics.

Flowers bloom
at the break of day;
stars scintillate
the evening sky;
oh, my sensitive poet,
where are thou!

The summer, rains, winter
and autumn by rotation
delivers poetic offerings to you
through wings of seasons.

This bouquet of tearful songs,
my heart's outpouring
I dedicate to you.

*A departed Odia poet of eminence.

A LONELY STORY

Quietly, once I wrote a lonely story
whose imagined form
still eludes me;
quietly this river flowing
beneath the sweeping Kashatandi
had kissed my heart's blue margin
many a time and returned.

Life dwindles thus ruminating the past
it is better to wind up
each one's tale quickly,
for none will live here long
to share the sorrows of life;
traces alone will lie behind.
All such solitary tales
always dissolve
at the back of attendant dreams.

Here, life is agonizing;
its image tearful, graphical,
simple and fluid;

but you are a quiet story,
defies comprehension
yet, I keep on writing for you
impassionately, only for you.

You are a lonely tale,
be it in verse or prose,
I have conferred you life;
my life is crowned.

A SONG FOR SEASONS

Be it rain, autumn or winter,
song of wind soothes the grey liner.

Bright sunshine on the bed of sand,
hope in plenty in shop of despair.

None knows who sells, who buys,
only a feeble memory lingers on.

Streak of light below the solid gloom,
who has sensed the dews' doom?

Every moon may be sweet and lovely,
but all are not food for love.

Who is dearer than the season
that shares the heart with others?

Vessel-like clouds may spark off rain
but worthless, if fail to yield a poem.

SURRENDER

The quiet abandon
of the hermit
swallows up life,
as sharing and caring
turn alien,
bond of love loosens,
aeons dwindle
as time goes by.

What a calm and collected earth,
an amazing mystery !
yet, one is fated to vanish
in the uneding search
through rotations of time.
The quest exudes venom,
oozes nectar too.

Man's yearning is a colossal ocean
eagerly waiting to embrace
myriad rivers.
Some merge into sea
trekking their paths
after many a meanndering;
and some others
get lost
in the wilderness of sand.

LIFE PETERING OUT

Very often, I feel
life petering out,
the visible frame becoming
charcoals and ashes
amid patches of green.

Life is petering out,
as I fail to gather
bits of dream and reality,
poetic lines on loss and guilt.
Life is petering out
eluding my search for life.

What do we mean by living
with so much desire !
Enough is enough.
Now, the time is up;
let us wind up
books of knowledge;
the pallid words packed
with grief
must one day end up
with life.

THE WANING HOUR

When the waning hour comes
shadows return,
sun sinks, stars blink.
gloom seizes the earth;
life's accounts get settled
with myriad images, figures, characters;
debates, dog fights
all melt away.

Time will tell the story
finally to everyone,
how well one has played the assigned role,
how easily drank life's cup of melancholy.

You and I will be no more here,
The timeless Time will go on moving
in whirling motion
and this waning hour will only keep on
recording the saga of human beings
for eons on end.

THE ROLE

Multiple postures and gestures
captivate birds, animals, sky and forest;
the singing river knowing no joy, no sorrow;
its etherial limits arrests my soul;
dark night goes hunting for someone,
who knows, who is the paramour!

Like a new bride in scarlet
vacillates on bed of grass,
someone forgets the way sometimes
and suffer.

The world is only a place,
for give and take, where
in the jostle to win
man gets hurt.
Life is a jungle housing
envy and malice,
yet conceals the key
to love and goodwill.

Man is always crazy
for life eternal, vies with Time,
soars the sky, writes songs for life
along the cloud, moon and stars
and reveals some secret misdeeds
whose outcome will be realised
in a far-off zone
amid the invisible hide and seek.

Each soul would echo
the plentive notes of a clarinet;
no one can sense
who plays which tune
in what raga of which song.

Like a tiny lamb,
the soul will go restless;
sin and merit will come out
black and white.
Time will flow on forever;
whose role comes after whom
will be known to none.

THE SOLACE

When sorrow weighs me down,
I gaze at poetic lines,
wishing the dumb words
cheer me up.
Briskly, they appear
like friends huddling around me,
talk and sing
pat my back and assure me:
"Don't bother,
the storm will pass,
grief will vanish.
Tricks and treachery will never trouble
a tranquil being.
Look!
how tidal waves sweep
the rivers and shores,
cascading rocks
pounding the foothills.
If they could endure,
why do you fear ?
you are no less !
you are colossal,
you are immense!"

INDIFFERENCE

You may disregard
everything :
deadly hunger, killer thirst,
charm of illusion, sheen of splendor;
but a spark of smile
or a breaking heart,
you can't ignore.

Hence, I keep on trekking
a long, lingering path
only to peruse that book,
the grammer of life,
the moving record
of soul's journey
beginning with a brook
ending in sea.

THE RIVER OF WISHES

The river is naive,
gullible too;
she even does not know
how far she has to take
to meet the sea.

Her friends are many.
Stars greet her,
wayside hills caress her;
she dances her way to the shore;
the loitering sea embraces her.

She has been silently watching
all that happen
on each of her islets;
the rustling wind,
scented Kia, Ketaki
stirring up dreams
in young sweet hearts.
At times, river sheds tears
on human follies
on foiled passion.
Man never knows

the end of his tether ;
river too fails to guess
her own age.
One who tries to sense the life
is eluded forever.

HISTORY

In the silence of night
someone lies in wait
like a lonely river.

The mountain musing with open lips
gazes at sky;
the remote soul mate
beckoning for a secret union.
Time passes quickly,
only the wait prolongs.

Young bosom sunk in grief
needs a caring one
along the blind alleys;
the path is puzzling.

Myriad tales were told;
some heard,
some went unheard.
Now, time is up ;
everything is history.

Who enters, who exists
nothing is chronicled,
History is only a dead pytheon
lies down as ever.

THE OMNISCIENT

Who has the guts to walk over
the formidable Time,
to wage war on Eternity,
to forge immortal lines
of infinite varieties?
He is the poet, none else;
a great sustainer of values,
precious in life.

Poet is the orb of seven sages.
The life present and lives to come
are manifest in his poems.
He is omniscient, ever present ;
a dream, a star, a moon,
never dies.
His soul watches only
the parading of successive lives.

■

LIFE AT THE TAIL END

Now a days, I feel
life fizzling out.
Of course, it takes a break
in pensive moments
when sobs and tears
stir up the heart,
but again gets going
with self-consolation.

The lamp of life
starts flickering.
I feel life slipping fast
in to a quick sand,
a magical snare.
I am caught unawares by life;
I am yet to know,
why it began,
why it ends.
Yet, I cling to life
like a charmed being.

If end of life is an escape;
a passage on to the divine;
why should I panic ?

NO ANSWER

What a hazardous toil
man takes on
nothing knowing
the chronicle of Time !

He boasts of
overturning the earth at will
by the flick of a finger;
revels in lots of fun and feats
flaunting myriad costumes
but is unaware;
his life is not worth a moment.

What a tussle
writing a book
on loss and gain !
No one cares to know;
the page of life will turn in a while;
life will dry up soon
like the last drops of summer rain.

Man is busy playing the end game.
If asked, "what next?";
No answer.

THE CAUTION

A ghost of fear
born of caution and experience
haunts the intimate bond
of light and darkness
and wrecks my unyielding faith.

I offered her a palmful of jasmine,
she chopped off my hand
fearing I would write a poem.
Poem, a sharp dagger
is the fiercest lady
on earth,
who records
the muddled history
of each and everyone secretly.

Yet, someone has already resumed
sowing seeds of follies and failings
on the sweet earth
undaunted and unnoticed.

THE HUG

Much of my life
I lost in chasing
a lovely moon
and sweet dreams.

The other day
I praised the ocean
for ravishing beauty;
the waves laughed gallantly
and packed me
with thousand doubts,
unending grief.

As the sea burst out laughing
my entire self plunged in grief
even though I knew:
decline is definite,
the way the full moon
weakens bit by bit.
Yet, why the moon stirs up
so much feeling and experience
causing recording of life's narrative!
The past turns into a mirror

clear and bright.
Moon seems to recite poems,
love and longs for more and more,\
listening to poems pricking up ears
as the dews drop from heaven,
kiss the sandy beach while
it hugs the moon-lit sky.

THE NOTICE

What a toil!
I lost count of times
I tried and failed
to win you over;
still, I am clueless
to get at your song of life
that twitters like birds.

There is song on your lips,
lyric in eyes;
sensuous poems throng your book of life
only a bundle of emotions,
and doubtful virtues.

Still, I am clueless
yet, charmed with fancy
for upcoming lives.
Where is birth, where is the soul ?
Everything is missing
in a wrong calculation.
I have not ignored them,
their fake notices
to get at you ;
but the notice I stamped
for you holds the clue
to life eternal.

THE POETIC PERSON

The lure of sensual pleasure
pushes every other things
into the back yard.
Own shadow looks awful,
the psyche grows grim,
faith on life sinks
poetry perishes,
the poet in man grieves,
his tears turn sharper than torrents.

The world, a hideous jungle,
tempts the gullible poet for indulgence,
a disaster that may crush him
without warning.

THE HOUSE OF ILLUSION

An elegant life we earned
the fruit of our love's labour;
a dream house we won
with surround vegetation of multiple hues;
we, too, secured
unique roles to play,
to look into each other's eyes
and win amazing oneness.

Blood has the tale of blood;
the tale that blooms in blood
never fades out from heart.

Alas! who told such a tale,
sang such a song!
only ruins and wrekage,
deckay and doom.
What a delusion !

The precious life leased to us
after so many births
we could not keep with care ;
the charmed house we loved so dearly
couldn't make our own.

Now you are summoned back
to the original home and gone.
The house of illusion
lies as it is.

ROLE PLAY

Moon stirs the garden of love,
charms young hearts
while stars blink
and tall casuarinas look on quietly.
Little carps are at play
in the village pond ;
on the bank a tombstone, below it
running steps of stone.

Night alights
hurling all the anguish
on to the rippling water ;
a bird hiding in a bamboo bush
starts singing a doleful song,
very difficult to follow.

Who, what for spills venom
on the lovely earth?
Why one longs to live to so long
only humming out false tunes ?
Why man brags and boasts
playing a fictitious role?

He is only a tiny dot in the great void.

No one will be here, in a moment;
all will pass into nothingness.
No one will remember
that someday, someone
was playing such a role
so subtle and elaborate.

THE TOUCH

The ordeal continues
even after much sizzling in sorrow.
Tests go on reminding again and again:
"Hard time is the essence of life."

When danger checkmates
along the perilous journey of life,
someone is always close on our heels
with a blanket to cover us,
to redeem us of guilt and sin.

Fear cann't rock
a virtuous fellow
but to err is human;
passions swell till
quenched completely.
sin and guilt cling to us
for ever and ever.

"End of desire ends suffering"
is, thus, too sacred
for human beings.

MOMENT TO MOMENT

Life appears and fades
like the breeze
playing hide-and-seek.
A flourishing bloom amuses all,
no one cares for the wilting one.
Amazing is the tide of time,
its origin known to none.
Yet, all are euphoric
like the cat that got the cream,
assuming life will not cease so soon,
the span is long and widening.

Like ink sinks through blotting paper,
life is squeezed into infinity,
turns anonymous.
Things remembered and then forgotten,
only, the priceless survives.

Time is hurtling ahead
from one station to the other.
passengers getting in and out hurriedly
as if a house on fire.

Nothing matters to the weaving bird;
the nest is tossing in the wind.
Gallant Time laughs derisively,
loudly proclaiming moment to moment:
Time knows no age, no end.

PYRAMID

Millions of pyramids
have raised their heads over generations
only to be covered with
dust of history.

Millions of blue fairies
have arrived on wings of seasons
and settled down to write
on heroic endeavours hidden by time.

Bosom sinks as grief marauding
like a locomotive
through mountain range.

Fountains lead to river,
rivers slip in to sea.
Life, too, is treading on thorny path,

battered and bruised,
falling, again rising,
still fighting back
with relentless Time.

Man may lose
and break his tiny wings,
estate of life may bleed;
passions will bloom afresh,
the flame of life
will glow beyond death
for Time to witness.

SALUTING THE CENTURY

Gale's fatigued body
rolled on the courtyard
of golden morning ;
the tender sun shining like
magic glaze of scaly fish
sprang up and opened
infinite varieties
onto the sweet earth.

Century arrived
hopping over another century,
tucking away
myriad joys and sorrows
events, accidents
of decades gone by.
The same way
the bygone century must have
arrived one day
narrating the opening tale.
My essence, by then,
won't have formed in to a dot.
How the earth was,
who the people were,

everything is beyond my grasp,
thus, it signifies nothing to me.

One day, in a fine morning,
another century will surface
with the rising sun.
I would be no more then
to partake in the joys and sorrows
of my fellow beings.

Tell me, therefore
how precious this century
is for me, for the earth, for humanity.
Let the flame of my life
finish off with that knowledge.

THE SELF

The primal desires when team up
river of grief swells
and enters the consciousness;
someone drawing near
whispers in the ear:
Does the soul dwell anywhere
outside the body
before divine communion!

Pathos can't wish away
the self, the weaver of sweet songs
for life.
Rise and ruin
union and separation
are only elemental
to human beings.

Why, then, is the false quest!
The ash grey darkness
might have set foot already
within you and me
without our knowledge.
But, no need to fear.

Darkness is, our own space
for winning hearts
in loving thoughts.
The self is ready for revealing now
the meaning of life in full
squeezed in a microdot.
True knowledge will melt
all our grief,
regret for defeat.

AMID THE SCENTED SEASONS

Amid the scented seasons
I lost my song book,
my sweet heart,
the record of my love
fresh as fragrance.

Words manifest
silence of dawn,
beauty of morning;
but all grief within
lie untold
for someone immolates
for seasons
and only for seasons,
the soul bird sings alone,
no audience to listen.

Seasons arrive and flee
as you yourself flew.
then, why such a thrill
in my heart
for seasons !

The sweet smell of seasons,
I have already drunk,
my soul turned aromatic for ever.
Life begins with season,
and ends with season.
In seasons lie the last trace of my being.

SHRI TAPAN PATTANAIK
THE POET

Shri Tapan Pattanaik born to late Padma Charan Pattanaik and Satyabhama Pattanaik on 8 June 1951 is a native of Balugaon located on the picturesque shoreline of Chilika lake in the district of Khordha, Odisha (India). His tender mind was first stirred into creativity by his poet and playwright father. Later, he grew among great Odia literary masters like Krushna Chandra Tripathy, Radhamohan Gadnaik, Dr. Mayadhar Mansingh and Sachi Routray whose inspirational presence instilled in him a deep devotion to life in literature. Nature, too, played a significant role in shaping his poetic mind and mission. The serene Gopalpur sea beach near Chamakhandi, the pastoral beauty of his maternal village Padmabati and the multihued Chilika lake nestling a birds' paradise quickend his literary sensibilities. As one of the most prolific and versatile Odia writers continuously writing for over five decades, he has produced a hamper of forty precious publications covering almost all forms of literature. He is, at the same time, a poet, lyricist and novelist. However, poetry is a passion for him. Love for life and nature pitted against an unheeding Time and elusive Destiny has been a recurrent theme of his poems, which he writes in free-flowing lyrical lines with a spontaneity rarely found in contemporary Odia literature. His prime resolve is to move forward, keep on writing nonstop and to embrace and capture each and every moment of life in its intensity and to preserve them in the immortal pages for posterity.

DR. NAMITA LAXMI JAGADDEB
THE TRANSLATOR

A native of Bahada (Khandapada), Dist-Nayagarh (Odisha), **Dr. Namita Laxmi Jagaddeb** has been serving as a lecturer in Deptt. of English, Mahima Degree College, Bijapali, Jharsuguda, Odisha (India) since 1997. She writes poems in Odia and English on a variety of themes, marked for elegance in style and intimacy of appeal. She also translates Odia poems into English and English poems into Odia. Her poems appear in the literary journals of the State as well as in International anthologies. She is associated with "Rock Pebbles", a UGC approved, peer reviewed journal of language and literature as Chief Sub-Editor. She is a Life Member of FSLE, India (A Chapter of ASLE-USA); Balavanta Parekh Centre for GS & HS, Baroda; Osmania University Centre for International Programmes, Hyderabad and Honorary Member of the Editorial Board of IJBST Group of Journals. She is also an official member of World Nations Writers' Union, Kazakhstan, which conferred upon her International Diploma, 'TEMIRQAZYQ- the Best Poet-Writer of the World, 2018' and 'World Laureate in Literature-2018'. She has been awarded Bharat Ratna Indira Gandhi Gold Medal in 2018 by GEPRA (India). She has been participating and presenting Research Papers in different National and International Seminars and Conferences in India and abroad. Recently, she has received the Biyotkesh Tripathy Best Paper Award (Runners Up) in the International Conference on Performing the Nation, 2019, organized by Berhampur University.

www.ingramcontent.com/pod-product-compliance
Lightning Source LLC
Chambersburg PA
CBHW060459080526
44584CB00015B/1479